DURABLE GOODS

Durable Goods

JAMES POLLOCK

THE POETRY IMPRINT AT VÉHICULE PRESS

Published with the generous assistance of the Canada Council for the Arts and the Canada Book Fund of the Department of Canadian Heritage.

 Canada Council   Conseil des arts
for the Arts   du Canada

SIGNAL EDITIONS EDITOR: CARMINE STARNINO

Cover design by David Drummond
Photograph of the author by Stormy Stipe
Set in Minion and Filosofia by Simon Garamond
Printed by Livres Rapido Books

Dépôt légal, Library and Archives Canada and the Bibliothèque national du Québec, third trimester 2022

LIBRARY AND ARCHIVES CANADA CATALOGUING IN PUBLICATION

Title: Durable goods / James Pollock.
Names: Pollock, James, 1968- author.
Description: Poems.
Identifiers: Canadiana (print) 20220258392 | Canadiana (ebook) 20220258449 | ISBN 9781550656107 (softcover) | ISBN 9781550656169 (HTML)
Classification: LCC PS8631.O455 D87 2022 | DDC C811/.6—dc23

Published by Véhicule Press, Montréal, Québec, Canada
www.vehiculepress.com

Distribution in Canada by LitDistCo
www.litdistco.ca

Distribution in the U.S. by Independent Publishers Group
ipgbook.com

Printed in Canada on FSC certified paper.

For my wife, Stormy Stipe,
and our son, Felix Pollock-Stipe

In memory of my mother,
Irene (Helberg) Pollock (1925–2020),
and my sister,
Nancy Pollock (1954–2018)

CONTENTS

Book

The book remembers living in the wood,
roots in the earth, wet boughs in the sky.
Perhaps if what is written here is good,
it may forgive the chainsaw. So to die

for hinge and board and flyleaf, sheaves of word,
dry heaven in which the silverfish believes—
or strange grove in which the author is a bird
and the reader the fresh wind that turns its leaves.

Gooseneck Lamp

Peering over your shoulder at your book
like a curious moon, its cone of light
blue as moonlight on the page, its long neck
craned attentively, as if to write

itself into the story you are reading,
the lamp, for all its brilliance, is discreet,
silent in fact, and placid in its pleading.
Only by degrees do you feel its heat.

Ceiling Fan

Seen from below, a white five-petal flower;
in fact, an artist whose medium is air,
who combs it with these pale palette knives, hour
on hour, stirring the room, spinning with care

to keep this slow whirlpool in circulation.
It gives you the chills, like an erotic spouse.
If you ramp up the speed of its rotation
it starts to imagine it could lift the house.

Faucet

This poet can convey the subtlest grades
of feeling, from iciness to scalding
or steamy fervency and all the shades
of warmth and lukewarmth in between, blending

intensity from the slow drip of tears,
from joyous gushing, from the spluttering
and gasping when the water disappears.
The truest poem is the most pretending.

Spectacles

Arms folded on the desk. They're skeptical,
aloof. They have their own way of seeing
things that is slightly off, not magical
exactly, but somehow mind-bending

in the way they turn the world, if not to
their will, at least away from the world's will,
if the world may be said to have one: true
visions, achieved through speculative skill.

Mirror

Only the precise truth in every part?
Look again: words are spelled backward, and letters
reversed; right and left have changed places; art,
or let us say realism, fetters

itself to reality in vain. No
gate to some other world; a perfect lie,
not least because it frames what we can know.
Why not just tell the truth? The truth is why.

Teaspoon

Its concave-convex bowl a funhouse mirror,
or two, in which the world appears upright
and upside down, and melting, in two blear
and mad illusions made by turning light,

as in an œil de sorcière. Of yore
a status symbol, now a drudge, this bold,
stirring measurer does what it's for,
immersed in cups of molten bronze and gold.

Dehumidifier

Ugly as a brutalist courthouse
with no windows. And silent. In the fog,
it starts to buzz in waves, a slaughterhouse,
or the irregular chorus of the bullfrog,

which will eat anything. By way of proof,
see how, when it chews the air, the fog clears,
little by little, to reveal the truth.
Inside, it keeps its reservoir of tears.

Barometer

It knows how much pressure you've been under,
that you could use a change of atmosphere.
Your seasonal depressions, rain and thunder,
are easier to predict than they appear.

But how long can you bear this cloudy heap,
under this weather, this black gloom, this despair?
Will it crush you in your fitful sleep
before the rising pressure clears the air?

Scale

To bear what it has to—that is the craft.
Also, to measure the force by which the world
brings one down. Imagine if it laughed
every time its inner dial got whirled,

bearing the unbearable. Which describes
how it does justice. It's a bit uncouth.
It lends you gravitas precisely when your scribe's
heart is weighed against the plume of truth.

Oscillating Fan

Consider this time-lapse sunflower in a cage,
chrome heliotrope searching gravely for
a god. It whirrs its blurry fins to assuage
its claustrophobic swivelling, with a snore

like the low fluttering of finches' wings.
How lovely this nuzzling breeze that blows slow-
ly. And yet, from side to side, the head swings
as if to say, sadly, *no*. And again, *no*.

Television

This medium, who sees phantoms at a distance—
and reveals them to you upon demand—
channels all she can, with the assistance
of one remote control to guide the hand.

The full depth of the trance all this induces—
transfixing the eye with what it views—
depends on the emotion it produces.
And on how much grief one has to lose.

Window

Before the photograph, there was the window:
one human perspective turning dim
infinity into this moving show,
like an external eye. All things that swim

the outer air in sun and rain and wind—
flies and whirling leaves, cardinals, dust, and bats—
are locked out by the window, and their sound
muffled, their scents kept at bay, since that's

the way a window brings the view inside,
as something especially to be seen,
and from this perspective, and as outside,
and in all weathers. It is not a screen

on which to view the contents of a camera,
but a frame for figuring the heart
in the seasons' changeable ephemera.
The window is itself a work of art.

Toilet

This clear pool in which the white winter sun
of a ceiling light appears: cold glacier
meltwater. Then the wan face of someone
haloed peering up at you from under.

Long *sploosh* and the puddle begins to spin,
small mad whirlpool, then disappears, almost,
with a stuttering gurgle. And again
that trembling, holy image of the ghost.

Kettle

Listen, it's haunted. Quavery metal *ping*,
clunk, then a long tense silence. This hiss. Low
or, rather, distant, banging or ratcheting
noises like basement renovations. Slow,

sustained sighs, growing hoarse. Huge pause for breath.
Hesitant whistles. Then this wheezing laugh,
growing hysterical, like a dance-of-death
devil's tritone, toggling on a fife.

At last, that throat-clearing rasp, low and long,
of hot water boiling, and a jet of steam
whose high crazy glissando plainsong—
poltergeist shrieking a baby's scream.

Scissors

First-class double lever with a pivot
fulcrum: blades, rivet, bows, and finger tang,
right- or left-handed. It lives to slit
paper, fabric, flesh, or wire, or hang

crosswise above a cradle, as you wish.
Crunch-chirp, crunch-chirp goes the bird; it lilts.
(Chalk is no shears.) In use: gar killing a fish.
En pointe: twins, conjoined, walking on stilts.

Washing Machine

Weighs your duds with joggles, with brief whirls.
Satisfied, locks the glass door with a click
that says, *Leave.* Poured water hisses, steam curls
to fog the window. Such work's on the clock.

Later you hear a crazy racket from
the basement: gush of water from a hose,
rhythmic churn, the unbalanced pounding of a drum.
Someone's beating the shit out of your clothes.

Vacuum Cleaner

Omnivore, dust addict. Boschian demon:
chrome tube head, hose neck, face all hairy mouth,
all mad roar. The *thwip* of things sucked up in.
The whine when what gets past its bristle teeth

sticks in its gizzard. Hot blast of rude air
out its rear. And, inside, this packed gut bag:
dead skin, staples, pennies, pubic hair—
detritus of one long voracious drag.

Mousetrap

"'Tis a knavish piece of work, but what o' that?"
–Hamlet

It's going to snap. But for now, it just kills
time, high-strung, tongue-tied, sitting tight among
floor crumbs. How can it not give you the chills?
A little peanut butter on its tongue.

Whole divisions deployed all over town,
assigned to be assassins of the mouse.
The coiled spring that brings the hammer down
has one thing to say: *Death is in the house.*

Pocket Knife

The pocket knife is given to reflection—
not so unbalanced as some might believe—
on that fine line between tool and weapon
to which knives, by design, are thought to cleave.

It's guarded. No, it won't be blunt just yet.
Steely, in fact, acute, lest you misuse
your knowledge of what it's keen on and won't whet
that precious edge it's so afraid to lose.

Vase

It literally can't keep its mouth shut—
speaks the colourful language of the flowers,
in which the pain and death of being cut
charges them with such suggestive powers.

Even alone, remembering the slaughter
turned by design into a bright tableau,
flat footed, up to its neck in water,
its upturned mouth forever saying O.

Lawn Mower

Keep clear of this single-minded editor
laying the damp cut blades in long green rows.
It keeps the grass down. It's a leveller.
Its mission is the only thing it knows.

Sprinkler

Not a sun- but a rain-dial, it tells time
rapidly, then untells it back again
like a rotary phone or pantomime
time machine. It pays to listen when

it stutters *T-*, *T-*, like a furious squirrel
outraged you let your garden get so dry.
Safer to stand back and watch it whirl
its turret machine gun, firing at the sky.

Umbrella

In photography, liturgy, or martial arts.
Or architecture. Or else for throwing shade,
to overshadow. The sum of its parts,
from ferrule to handle, times how it's made:

pole, stretchers, ribs, and canopy. Courage
to learn, like a character in a novella,
when it rains or shines, to take, not umbrage,
but cover, under a sombre umbrella.

Lock

The steel tongue is my front door's strongest part.
It's exacting, and will not let me pass
without my matching key, whose phallic art,
entering the keyway of its brass

case plug, lifts the springs, each in its own shaft,
so the driver pins, like zinc teeth on a comb,
line up with the shear line. For such craft,
such rapture, the lock opens. I am home.

Pencil

Middle English for "fine paintbrush," from Old French
pincel, from a diminutive of Latin *peniculus* ("brush"),
diminutive of *penis* ("tail")

Hard graphite shaft in a smooth hexagonal
incense-cedar casing. Since it is sex
its name alludes to, so the work of all
its lacquer, ferrule, factice, pumice, wax,

its clay-and-crystalline-carbon abrasions,
its rubber erasures, is at last to crown
its breaking point with lusty lineations—
though what keeps it sharp can be what grinds it down.

Coffee Grinder

Like a power tool or an artisan,
it does one perfect thing. You rattle your
half cup of beans into the epicurean
hopper and turn it on. It starts to roar

and grind, harsh as a tree chipper, and when
most of that handful has been ground up, the pitch
rises like a tornado siren,
and one last hard seed starts to reel and twitch

about the inverted cone, trying not
to get crushed in the whirling burrs. Turn it off
and there's a disappointed whine, sad thought
of loss ending in a gravelly cough.

Reach down and snap out the fragrant chamber,
full to the brim of what we'll soon be drinking,
and measure out some coarse grains of burnt umber
mixed with brown madder grounds that smell like thinking.

Dryer

This seemingly permanent revolution,
this engine turning over endlessly,
full of metallic bonks, clatter of button,
and a low rumbling burden, lets us see

its wry internal rough-and-tumble—arms
and legs like wrestlers or fierce fighting dogs,
wet, leaping, twisting in mid-air, blurred forms
plunging in and out of knots that flog

themselves and radiate more heat than light—
lets us see it all through this round porthole
window to the inner life, this insight
too true, however dry, however droll.

Refrigerator

Compartmentalizing is its super-
power. Everything inside has its cool
dry place, from the egg tray to the crisper,
like an office building or a school,

albeit at slightly varying temperatures,
from chill to chilly—dryly humorous
in their juxtapositions, their postures,
their unspoken hierarchies from serious

to silly. Then, every so often,
the door swings open and a light comes on
and reveals the truth: some things are going rotten,
some are running low, and some are gone.

Stove

All cool and clean in the quiet kitchen.
Some annoyed snapping, and blue flames leap up
with a whoosh, in circles, in sequence, then
settle down to precise licking. My cup,

my French whip, my ring of spoons, my pans
whirl over the elements in a cloud
of steam, a rain of flour, a blur of hands,
and little explosions of oil as loud

as cap guns. Now the boiling point approaches:
the milk scalds, the cast iron sears the meat,
the sauce simmers, and the egg, perfect, poaches.
And, inside the oven, a silent growing heat.

Microwave

It takes your cold cup in like a new thought,
shines a light on it, turns it slowly around.
It's circumspect. Begins to meditate
on your maximum mug. (That humming sound

you hear is *om*.) But what is observed is
changed in the act of observing it,
in this case, at least, which means the vessel does
warm to the attention, though let's admit

it isn't personal. The ragout gains
bouquet, softens, augments in piquancy,
acquires (recovers, rather) colour, strains
in each morsel with the exigency

of inward heat, lets off some steam, and pops.
The machine emits a long obnoxious bleat,
and all goes dark. The transformation stops.
The truth is, it's not too beautiful to eat.

Radio

Has no privacy. You can read its mind
or, rather, hear the voices in its head,
whether muse or madness or the two combined,
the hiss of multicoloured noise or dead

silence. Turnabout—since it rings those clear tones
of talk and music in your own hemispheres—
is fair play. Whence it batters the small bones—
forges, with hammer and anvil, in your ears.

Ultrasonic Humidifier

Slender as a black ashcan or giant
tube of lipstick, upturned face a gold-ring
orifice like a damned and defiant
diva singing O so high (does she sing

or is this screaming?) no one but the dog
can hear her. A continuous stream of mist
blows upward like a searchlight of white fog
or power station smokestack. If you insist,

the fan whirrs wanly. It looks effortless.
But, if you look closely—and what fears
shake her diaphragm we can only guess—
you can see some drops of sweat, or are they tears?

Dishwasher

Again the maestro is preoccupied.
A distant march of salvaged instruments
circles the square: harmonium; cockeyed
tinpot drumkit clatter; dissonance

of sousaphone, of whooshing cymbals; bass
drum thud; the drone of bagpipes so far off
the long waltz wavers. Listen harder: grace
notes, pinging, overtones, relentless cough

of an offbeat tom-tom underneath
the faintest plainsong of the human voice
invoking, *Sing*. For three hours in the teeth
of silence in the kitchen, then, rejoice,

musician, in the mournful lento blast
of trumpets echoing, in this crazed assault
on indifferent death itself—until, at last,
your whole thing, sighing, shudders to a halt.

Sewing Needle

All eye and backbone and piercing toe.
Stiff paleolithic archetype of skill,
sine qua non of duds—we make it go
up and down, over and under, until

the taut line pulls the stitches tight. We fasten,
whence, like a sine wave, the way grows eternal.
It is the longing of the eye: to fashion,
whereby the fashioner makes the self external.

Briefcase

This devoted vehicle to which you're married
brims with what it tries to convey,
the tenor of which is that it gets carried,
when it can't contain itself, away.

Of all bags, it's the best to be left holding,
an outward carryall of inward space.
Often, it carries the day in its unfolding
out of everything that, oddly, is the case.

Elevator

Precisely because it understands
the gravity of your situation
and, what's more, why you're making these demands,
it opens up to you. It takes you in

despite, or because of, the way you push
its buttons. And always, to show its worth,
to comfort you, it closes with a hush.
It's uplifting. Then it brings you down to earth.

Paper Clip

Easily bent out of shape. Still, it bends over
backward, in loops of steel wire, to help you hold
not just on, frankly, but it together—
attaché that, with torsion and twofold

elasticity in the steel, grips better
than mere friction of its tongues alone.
In a pinch, barrette, lock pick, screwdriver.
Or: Circus Maximus, Lilliputian trombone.

Screw

Spiral staircase, or ramp, rather, as in
a tiny parking garage, or the shoots
of the scarlet runner—such things as spin
a helix, one of nature's absolutes,

into the matrix of the universe.
Turn the self-locking vortex by the head
with your torquing driver; such tight verse
holds all things together by a thread.

Ruler

Rules against no one. Rules nothing out (or in).
Unlike Man, is not the measure of all things.
It only wants to know where to begin
to measure out the line. It only brings

some rhythmical proportion to the space.
About the facts, it's rigid—keeps them straight—
puts its foot down in a righteous place
beyond measure, in which one may create.

Framing Hammer

A brute. A hard- and heavy-headed banger,
it's true. And yet one that articulates
the architecture. Steelhead T. Clawfinger
V: the consonants it enunciates

when nailing and, later, removing nails,
plosive and fricative. For such a head,
not flying off the handle still entails
squarely applying force to what is said.

Saw

The panel saw on its hook, like a rag of map,
its blade an obtuse triangle of plain,
its serrated edge a sierra. Scrap
of landscape lush with spirits of the slain.

It's skilled at long division and, like the law,
separates what is good from what is true.
That's the Cartesian wisdom of this old saw
for whom one divided by one is two.

Compass

This clock for telling space turns your attention
to the way you're going, which is all it knows.
It can't point you in the right direction
or make you decide to box the compass rose.

Though born as a device for divination,
it never points its finger at true north.
It only tries to tell you, by gyration,
more than what you knew in setting forth.

Flashlight

Nothing is braver. Darkness its element,
its gear a diode, batteries, a case,
a switch, a focus, and a temperament
suited to detection in the face

of forgery. It finds lost things, keyholes,
targets, and the way, with photons hurled
at mystery. It understands its role is
to propagate some light into the world.

Pen

A rocket, pointed at an angle down
and filled not with liquid oxygen but ink.
It travels to the planets Verb and Noun.
It's just a simple tool with which to think.

The tiny steel ball bearing at the tip
rolls like a swirl-blue marble when you write.
It transmits one last message from the ship.
Then the Pilot disappears from sight.

Lighter

The hand-held Titan doffs his cap thus: *schling!*
A little sloshing in the belly. Wick,
spark wheel, eyelet, flint spring, chimney. Plaything,
the ancient miracle become a trick,

or many: Drop Spark, Bar Slide, Spinning Wheel,
The Married Man, The Twilight Zone, The Gun.
Who now remembers what it took to steal
this cunning tongue of fire from the sun?

Candle

The ruffled flame shudders like a spooked quail.
It ought, like a hummingbird, to hover
above the taper, that the light prevail,
the tight braid of the cotton wick curl over

like a finger. It shines a constant flame
on the table, gutters on the shelf,
pours scent like a half-forgotten name,
and makes light of, not suffering, but itself.

Wind Turbine

From afar, you see the world's most graceful
stick man demonstrating the backstroke.
In the gale, he stands like Lear, but thoughtful,
absorbing power as he moves, to invoke

the element, like Prospero, and argues
with the whirlwind in the darkest hours,
like Job. A tall poet breathing the Muse,
he transforms the windstorm into power's

currency, which cools the air in which I write,
and steadily, over my shoulder and from
the screen on which I type these words, shines light.
Make ready for the wind, and it will come.

ACKNOWLEDGEMENTS

I am grateful to the editors of the following journals where many of these poems first appeared, often in different versions.

The Antigonish Review: "Oscillating Fan," "Wind Turbine"
Event: "Toilet"
The Fiddlehead: "Framing Hammer"
Geist: "Barometer," "Flashlight," "Refrigerator," "Sprinkler," "Television," "Umbrella," "Washing Machine"
The Humber Literary Review: "Coffee Grinder," "Faucet," "Mirror"
Magma: "Gooseneck Lamp"
The Manchester Poetry Prize website and *Met Magazine*: "Lighter," "Scale," "Screw," "Sewing Needle"
Painted Bride Quarterly: "Ceiling Fan," "Spectacles"
Plume: "Dryer"
Southern Poetry Review: "Mousetrap"
The Walrus: "Kettle"

Warm gratitude to judges Mona Arshi, Malika Booker, and Mimi Khalvati for awarding "Lighter," "Scale," "Screw," and "Sewing Needle" the 2020 Manchester Poetry Prize.

I am grateful to final judge Frank Morgan for awarding "Mousetrap" the 2021 Guy Owen Prize from *Southern Poetry Review*.

Thank you very much to the editors of *Magma* for awarding "Gooseneck Lamp" the 2020 Editors' Prize.

And many thanks to the editors of *Painted Bride Quarterly* for discussing "Ceiling Fan" and "Spectacles" on the *Painted Bride Quarterly Slush Pile* podcast.

Thanks, as well, to Loras College for funding my participation in the Tupelo Press Manuscript Conference, which helped me improve the manuscript significantly.

I am profoundly grateful to my editor, Carmine Starnino, for his superb advice; to Jeffrey Levine, who read a version of the manuscript and made many excellent suggestions; to Derek Webster, who made several fine suggestions after reading one of these poems online; to Jonah Brunet, who copyedited the manuscript; to David Drummond, who designed the cover; and, above all, to my brilliant and beloved spouse, Stormy Stipe, who read and responded to every draft of the poems and of the manuscript, holding every line, word, and syllable to the highest standards.

Finally, many thanks to my publisher, Simon Dardick, and everyone at Véhicule Press.

Signal
EDITIONS

Peter Dale Scott • Deena Kara Shaffer
Carmine Starnino • Andrew Steinmetz • David Solway
Ricardo Sternberg • Shannon Stewart
Philip Stratford, trans. • Matthew Sweeney
Harry Thurston • Rhea Tregebov • Peter Van Toorn
Patrick Warner • Derek Webster • Anne Wilkinson
Donald Winkler, trans. • Shoshanna Wingate
Christopher Wiseman • Catriona Wright
Terence Young